Don't Date A Dick

A reality-based dating adventure

By Charles J. Orlando

Illustrations by Vanessa Villamizar

one room press

LOS ANGELES, CA

This book is an original publication of
One Room Press
A division of Loft 327, Inc.
333 S Grand Avenue, Suite 450
Los Angeles, CA 90071
oneroompress.com

ORP Paperback Edition 2017
10 9 8 7 6 5 4 3 2 1

1. Interpersonal Relations   2. Self-Esteem
3. Consciousness & Thought   4. Marriage & Adult Relationships

ISBN 0-9979029-0-6
ISBN-13: 978-0-9979029-0-7

Printed in the United States of America.

For women daters all over the world
who are tired of mixed messages,
dick pics, booty calls and bullshit.

There are great guys out there.
But to find them, you first have to
stop dating dicks.

This is Hope.

Hope dates guys who are dicks.

Hope met Tom online.
He took her on three dates.

NO orgasm
NO 4th date
NO nothing

After she slept with him, Tom ghosted on her.

Tom is a dick.

Malcolm, John, Andy, and
Phil all swiped right... and
then sent cock shots and
verbally-abusive messages.

They are all dicks.

Hope and Jeff dated for a year. But Jeff was hooking up with lots of other women behind Hope's back.

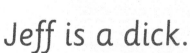

Jeff is a dick.

Hope thought Eddie was The One.
But so did his wife and kids.

Eddie is a dick.

Brad is Hope's ex.

    He comes by occasionally for a booty call.

                                                  Brad is a dick.

Hope hangs out with her friends.

They all date dicks, and they're all pissed.

Hope isn't mad. She's sad.
She thinks it's all her fault.

Hope just wants to love and be loved.
To respect and be respected.
To value and be valued.

One morning...

Sick of being sad..
    Finished with men...
        Tired from no sleep...

Hope reached for her trusty
   coffee mug, and for the first time...

...she <u>really</u> understood what was written.

Hope needed to WAKE UP and get into a new relationship right away...

...with herself.

It was time for Hope
to work on Hope.

Hope needed to find herself <u>first</u>...

...then, love would find <u>her</u>.

Hope surrounded herself
with positive people.

16

Hope did good things for her mind...

...for her body...

...and for her spirit.

Hope tried lots of new things.

Scared... but doin' it!

She was on the path to becoming her Best Self.

Then... Brad, Hope's booty-calling ex, showed up.

But Hope was prepared. She knew she was valuable, and dicks were not worthy of her time.

As dick after dick from her past popped up,
Hope declared her worth by casting them out.

By working on herself, Hope came to realize who was REALLY in control of her life...

Hope had de-dicked her life!

She found herself officially dickless!

With her improved self-worth, Hope had new challenges to face. Namely, what should she do with a guy who's not a dick?

Talking to a nice guy felt so unfamiliar.

Hope needed to check out his true intentions.

Hope was nervous.
She didn't want to get hurt again.

Hope knew there were no guarantees...

...but she also knew that she was worthy
and ready for someone who valued her.

Hope... found Hope.

ABOUT THE AUTHOR

. . . .

Charles J. Orlando is an interpersonal relations and relationship dynamics researcher who frequently goes undercover in the worlds of dating, marriage and infidelity. His center of study is the intersection where technology and love collide. His writing highlights his real-world experiences that bring to light the issues that plague modern-day relationships. Find out more about Charles on his website at charlesjorlando.com or on Facebook at facebook.com/charlesjorlando

Other Books By Charles J. Orlando

The Pact: Goodbye, Past. Hello, Love!

The Problem with Women... is Men®
The Evolution of a Man's Man to a Man of Higher Consciousness

The Problem with Women... is Men®: Volume 2 - A Social Media Memoir

CPSIA information can be obtained
at www.ICGtesting.com
Printed in the USA
BVOW05s0851090117
472981BV00017B/150/P